Servant Leadership

B. Vincent

Published by RWG Publishing, 2021.

SERVANT LEADERSHIP

First edition. July 8, 2021.

Written by B. Vincent.

Also by B. Vincent

Affiliate Marketing
Affiliate Marketing
Affiliate Marketing

Standalone
Affiliate Recruiting
Business Layoffs & Firings
Business and Entrepreneur Guide
Business Remote Workforce
Career Transition
Project Management
Precision Targeting
Professional Development
Strategic Planning
Content Marketing
Imminent List Building
Getting Past GateKeepers
Banner Ads
Bookkeeping

Bridge Pages
Business Acquisition
Business Bogging
Marketing Automation
Better Meetings
Conversion Optimization
Creative Solutions
Employee Recruitment
Startup Capital
Employee Mentoring
Servant Leadership

Table of Contents

Servant Leadership

R obert Greenleaf once said:

"The first and most significant decision A pioneer settles on is the decision to serve".

Furthermore, John C. Maxwell advises us,

"Individuals don't mind the amount you know, until they realize the amount you give it a second thought".

In the present age, it's gotten clear and uncontestable.

Worker Leadership is the new norm of authority. The world's top CEOs and originators apply it in their organizations. The world's most regarded authority specialists depend on it. In the event that a pioneer needs his association to dominate, he should be ready to put others first. As Ken Blanchard puts it, 'everything's tied in with making the objectives understood, and afterward focusing in and taking the necessary steps to assist with peopling win. In that circumstance, they don't work for you, you work for them'. In any case, how might we guarantee we're satisfying this new norm in our work environment? What's more, how might we best influence it to carry our association higher than ever.

In this course, we're demonstrating how to do precisely that.

79% OF WORKERS QUIT their positions because of an absence of appreciation. A pioneer not giving out clear bearings, not setting aside effort to plunk down with workers, and not giving customary input, were among the best 10 representative protests in the US.

Just 14% of CEOs have the initiative ability they need to develop their organizations. These measurements show that worker administration is an inexorably significant region that organizations should zero in on.

Our course will comprise of a progression of basic conversation focuses. These are intended to cover this wide point as altogether as could really be expected, to energize development in these crucial regions and to work with a genuine and productive conversation inside your association about how you can each enhance this fundamental trademark, both at work and in your own lives by and large.

A portion of these will be really protracted, and some will be somewhat clear and brief. At the finish of this guide, comes the main last advance.

Conversation time

Try not to skirt this. This is the main piece of this preparation.

At the point when you finish this course, you need to go through somewhere around an hour or so going over the inquiries we supply toward the end collectively. Whoever's the big enchilada in the gathering should assign a facilitator whose duty is that each question is covered and that everybody time allowing, can express their opinion. Ensure all commitments are esteemed, all ideas considered, and all assessments regarded.

So we should move into the principal conversation point.

Listen Attentively

Listening is the central nature of Servant Leadership. As a Servant Leader, you ought to normally have the craving of needing to serve others, you comprehend that the prosperity of your representatives is your main concern. You likewise perceive that they can give important contribution to the group. This is the reason correspondence is so significant in each business.

Listening is significant concerning their prosperity. A ton of representatives experience low assurance every now and then, it might originate from individual worries outside of work, for example, monetary or family issues.

Another underlying driver may be factors inside the workplace, like inclination wore out in work, or experience unseemly treatment from other staff.

Sometimes, they may encounter actual torment like ailment, or enthusiastic misery, similar to tension, or sadness. These components can profoundly influence their assurance in the working environment, and may prompt terrible showing. On the off chance that you saw somebody in your group who is feeling down or having a harsh day, why not welcome them to plunk down and talk things over? Try not to hang tight for them to come to you. Step up.

Obviously you probably won't be an authorized advisor, or a prepared master that can give proficient exhortation yet what's everything thing you can manage as a pioneer? Tune in, truly tune in.

Listen mindfully as they open up, don't interfere. Allow them to communicate openly what's in their brains. Take in the thing they're saying. You'll be amazed how a few group don't actually require answers for their issues. They simply need somebody to tune in. Be that somebody.

Show Empathy

Tuning in and showing compassion go inseparably. Listening is pointless in the event that it goes directly off of your mind. As you get things, according to their viewpoint, show compassion. Without being sincerely contributed, attempt to place yourself in their circumstance.

This will assist you with understanding things according to their point of view. This thusly can lead you to furnish them with the best commonsense assist that you with canning.

What are the other reasonable ways you can show sympathy in the work environment?

Consider utilizing these expressions the following time you go to work.

How are you feeling?

I would feel the same way.

How might I help? Inform me concerning it. Is there something incorrectly?

Practice Self-Awareness

A decent pioneer ought to comprehend the qualities and shortcomings of their representatives yet an incredible pioneer perceives their own positives and negatives as well.

Mindfulness is a fundamental quality each worker chief ought to have.

Mindfulness is characterized as being familiar with your qualities and character. You perceive that you're blemished, that you will in general have a frail point of view from specific things.

Mindfulness is such a significant characteristic that a pioneer ought to have, for it creates passionate knowledge. It assists you with recognizing your restrictions, and understand what things you need to chip away at to be a superior chief.

At the point when you're mindful of your attributes, propensities and feelings, and what your activities mean for other people, you will actually want to deal with your feelings and settle on better cool headed choices. This thus will propel others to do likewise.

What are simply the principal approaches to rehearse mindfulness? Think about these ideas. Take a character test.

Practice self-contemplation, set restrictions, know about your enthusiastic triggers, practice self-control, persuade utilizing influence.

Propel Using Persuasion

It's sensible for your workers to follow you since you're a chief. In any case, utilizing your position doesn't generally rouse them to make a move. You need them to feel that they're included and that their activities will add to the group's prosperity. You do that through influence.

At the point when we hear the word influence, perhaps the principal thing that flies to us is the demonstration of beguiling somebody, ordinarily by smooth deals strategies yet that is not the situation for Servant Leadership. To convince intends to alter somebody's perspective and persuade them to adjust their perspectives and activities. Dominating the Art of Persuasion is the way to being an extraordinary worker pioneer.

At the point when you carefully convince others, you urge them to make the right decision for the association.

Another motivation behind why Persuasion is significant is that it constructs agreement dynamic. At the point when a pioneer utilizes influence to decide, they can incite everybody to be in total agreement, and all the more significantly, that everybody upholds the choice made.

How might you foster influence?

Here are a couple of propensities that you should begin dealing with:

Foster Curiosity

Worker Leaders are curious in their general surroundings, and individuals they work with. Put forth an attempt to know the physical and feelings of every person. Become acquainted with what their fantasies and yearnings are. This will help you on the best way to convince them better.

Listen Attentively:

When conversing with one of your representatives, listen mindfully. Show individual interest by looking at them without flinching and utilizing their name all through your discussion.

Mindfulness shows that you esteem their assessment. suppositions that are esteemed and regarded. assist with building shared trust. This trust thusly will make it simpler for them to be convinced.

Practice Honesty:

The force of your influence and your believability as a pioneer is enormously influenced by the degree of trustworthiness you show to your group. Being unscrupulous can deceive them, and can harm the fellowship and your general standing.

As a Servant Leader, you ought to endeavor to be straightforward consistently, in any event, when reality harms. Eventually, individuals will see the value in genuine and impartial criticism.

Lead through Stewardship

A pioneer is benevolent and mindful. Pioneers are stewards. They're liable guardians that regulate and ensure their group. They continually search for ways on the best way to improve and grow the business. At the point when you lead through stewardship, you shape your association to greatness.

As a steward, you're focused on accomplishing the drawn out objectives of your organization by defining transient objectives, while staying ardent to the organization's guiding principle.

In spite of inward and outside pressures that they may experience, Servant Leaders stay patient and relentless in arriving at their destinations. How might you rehearse stewardship in your business?

Here are three fundamental ways:

Zero in on advancing prosperity:

As a pioneer, you need to ensure that everybody is content with their work. Discover approaches to make their work more charming.

Support Camaraderie:

Guarantee that everybody in your group associates well with each other. Endeavor to keep a sound collaboration in the working environment. Change hierarchical qualities when required. As globalization shapes organizations today, you need to ensure that your organization's basic beliefs are lined up with the developing society.

Set Expectations through Conceptualization:

Think ambitiously, reach skyward. These words characterize what conceptualization is. At the point when you conceptualize, you're zeroing in not on the present, but rather on what lies ahead later on.

Your central goal and vision are future situated and your destinations are constantly disposed to the not so distant future.

Conceptualization is anything but an individual journey. Maybe, it's worked around individuals who assist you with accomplishing those fantasies. To do that, worker pioneers should move toward singular work connections as long haul responsibilities. At the start of the relationship, assumptions ought to be set, giving them responsibility. At the point when representatives have possession to assist with forming the organization's vision, they will discover more reason and significance to their work.

Push Ahead Using Foresight

Firmly identified with conceptualization, Foresight is another attribute that a worker chief ought to have.

The explanation is that; we as a whole commit errors. Mistakes are inescapable, particularly according to a business point of view. Missteps can influence you, however you can utilize these as a learning experience for you to keep on developing.

Gaining from botches assist you with settling on a superior choice in the future however that is not all. Prescience glances previously, but at the same time is cautious to current circumstances. We see steady change each day.

Having foreknowledge, you ceaselessly search for ways on the most proficient method to develop your business by acquiring knowledge on at various times occasions, then, at that point extricating these snippets of data so you can keep on adjusting in this consistently evolving world.

Be Committed to the Employees Growth

As a pioneer, you comprehend that singular development is vital for aggregate advancement. You ought to be profoundly dedicated to sustaining their own and expert development. This can be through contributing time, cash, and assets to assist them with being adult as a laborer, yet in addition as a person.

What are a few different ways you can uphold their development?

Here are a couple of representative undertakings:

In the event that you have a great deal for you to deal with, why not delegate different duties to your group. This won't just save you additional time, yet additionally fosters their abilities.

Give out stretch tasks:

These are assignments past their present jobs and abilities. It's intended to allow them to consider new ideas, permitting them to extend formatively.

Presented new organizations:

As the top of the organization, you're in a situation to open entryways for making new associations with your representatives. Acquaint them with different experts, specialists and coaches. Extending their organization sets out a ton of open doors to get further help, information and guidance on the most proficient method to develop actually and expertly.

Carry out Job Shadowing:

Occupation shadowing is a movement where a staff from one space of the association has the chance to work close by other staff in various regions and gain understanding from the experience. You can utilize work shadowing to prepare people to work close by more experienced associates. So they can learn and develop inside their present job.

Set up Cross Training Programs:

This program prepares a worker to do an alternate piece of the association. This hands on approach further develops spirit, supports efficiency and advances development.

Express Appreciation

When was the last time you said much obliged? You might be so found work that you neglect to say a few expressions of appreciation to your dedicated representatives. Saying thank you isn't only some organization essential. Nor is it a simple commitment that supervisors ought to do. You give acknowledgment since you are appreciative. You voice out these expressions of appreciation, since that is the thing that your heart advises you to do.

Tragically, an absence of appreciation causes representatives to feel that their work doesn't make any difference, or that their endeavors are neglected. This brings down their confidence, and diminishes the degree of exertion they put into your organization. Whenever left untreated, you may wind up losing one of your top laborers.

As a pioneer, your responsibility is to communicate these expressions of appreciation consistently.

How might you show yourself grateful?

One way is by conversing with your workers individually, earnestly reveal to them the amount they intend to the group and how you esteem their endeavors.

Keep in mind, it doesn't need to be elegant and overstated. Short yet true signal is sufficient to get them in a good place again.

At the point when you routinely give out representative acknowledgment, you will expand usefulness, work fulfillment, worker bliss, maintenance, reliability, group culture.

Approach Employees with Respect

Regard is basic for worker authority. Treating representatives with poise adds to their prosperity. At the point when you regard representatives, they become more ready, inventive and useful, consequently bringing about a more certain work environment.

In this way, with regards to showing regard, consistently recollect, treat others the manner in which you need to be dealt with. You approach your workers with deference when you show: graciousness, generosity, and good manners.

Keep away from micromanaging rush to pass judgment, comprehend their restrictions, pay attention to their suppositions know about your non-verbal communication, manner of speaking and attitude. Treat them reasonably and similarly. Practice compassion, regard their way of life, and convictions.

Further develop Interaction in Meetings

In case you're a worker, there have been times that you may have felt awkward during a gathering. The explanation is that it appears to be that your sole responsibility is to tune in, tune in, and tune in.

Nonetheless, it's basic that each individual in the gathering should feel that their participation is advantageous and that their commitment is profoundly esteemed. As a Servant Leader, your responsibility is to make collaboration among the group.

How might you prod cooperation inside the gathering?

Think about these reasonable tips:

Support planning:

A decent tip for planning is to urge your participants to set up their inquiries ahead of time. During the gathering, request that they give refreshes or pose inquiries. A solid and steady request will most likely profit the entire group and will allow them to feel that they are fundamental.

Include everybody:

For facilitators, your responsibility is to ensure that everybody in participation ought to have an offer in the conversation. In the event that you have fresh recruits or alleged contemplative people, why not let them have a say. Allowing everybody an opportunity to communicate their contemplations implies that you esteem their assessments.

Taking an interest additionally permits them to see the value in the reason for such gatherings.

Engage different inquiries. With regards to partaking. Everybody has an alternate perspective. Some lean toward clear inquiries, while others need to handle applied issues.

Knowing this, you should make it a highlight approach such inquiries in a careful manner. Truth be told, you can start intriguing themes that can animate their psyches, bringing about an all the more profoundly intelligent gathering.

Offer Them a Reprieve

Now and again, you may discover that your laborers look bleak and discouraged. Furthermore, there could be various reasons why?

A few representatives feel that their work is only exactly the same thing again and again, as though being stuck in a perpetual circle.

Then again, somebody may be managing infection, loss of a friend or family member, relationship issues and other individual issue. Concerning others, they essentially can't deal with the pressing factor of their work, making them become worried and consumed.

As a worker chief, how might you keep them from being worn out?

Give them a breather. A vacation day from work and assist them with being invigorated and revived. At the point when they get back to work, they will feel more invigorated giving greater usefulness.

As a Servant Leader, how would you be able to deal with guarantee that they have sufficient balance between serious and fun activities, you ought to guarantee that your representatives reserve the option to take excursions. You can do this by applying a took care of time strategy. This approach just implies that a representative has the option to have downtime from work while as yet getting paid.

PTO's include: occasions, days off, get-away, and individual issue, for example, deprivation leaves, jury obligation, and surprisingly military preparing.

At the point when you apply PTO to your business, you give your workers the opportunity to take vacation days as per their circumspection. It likewise permits them to have some control of their timetable to go to individual issue. Sufficiently sure, workers will esteem the adaptability that they acquire through this arrangement. This is on the grounds that you give them the option to have a break when they would require it the most.

Foster Keystone Habits

The motivation behind why Servant Leadership is so powerful is that the pioneers have created Keystone propensities.

Cornerstone Habits, as characterized by Charles Duhaig are little changes, or propensities that individuals bring into their schedules that unexpectedly persist into different parts of their life.

As a worker chief, obtaining these allegorical propensities change you to be simply the best form, so you can serve more individuals better.

Here are a couple of instances of Keystone propensities:

- Daily work out.
- Sleeping early.
- Writing an every day diary.
- Cooking.
- Donating to good cause.
- spending quality time with friends and family.
- Meditation.
- Practicing appreciation.

These Keystone propensities fill in as building blocks and making a fruitful authority. These propensities fortify your physical, mental, and enthusiastic state, working on your government assistance.

Put out Smart Goals

Worker Leaders endeavor to make objectives that are secure. Tragically, not all objectives produce compensating results. It will consider plans or propensities that will just prompt a pointless pursuit. To accomplish your ideal outcomes. You need to make objectives that can create that sort of result. These objectives are classified "Brilliant Goals".

Building up Smart Goals make it simpler to imagine what achievement resembles. What does a Smart Goal mean?

Here's the breakdown:

S; Specific:

Keen Goals should be explicit, clear and obvious. Realizing your for what reason is the way to understanding your inspiration and will fuel you to remain focused. The more explicit and itemized the objective you set, the more probable it will be refined. At the point when objectives are not explicit enough, you set yourself up to fizzle.

M; Measurable:

Savvy Goals should have rules for measuring progress. By separating an objective to explicit measurements. You make your objective unmistakable, set useful propensities and examples, evaluate your advancement and realize when you've accomplished it.

Seeing gradual improvement towards an objective will likewise invigorate and spur you to keep with it and accomplish your objective.

A; Achievable:

To lay out the groundwork for yourself objectives should be feasible. This implies something outside of your usual range of familiarity, yet not so cumbersome that you set yourself up to fall flat. Objectives ought to give a design, yet additionally the adaptability.

R; Relevant:

Objectives should be applicable to your needs. Laying out an objective to run a long distance race when your most noteworthy dream is to compose a book isn't applicable. Ensure objectives line up with your fantasies and needs. Likewise, consider if accomplishing your objective will be in your control or if achievement will be directed by outer conditions.

T; Time Bound:

Put out cutoff times around your objectives so you can keep fixed on accomplishing them. Maybe than essentially laying out an objective of practicing or eating great.

Adding a cutoff time will make the objective more feasible. Cutoff times have the additional advantage of reflection. It permits time to survey progress, considering what worked and what didn't.

Foster a Sense of Urgency

A Servant Leader esteems time and makes the most out of consistently. This is the reason having a Sense of Urgency is indispensable for effectiveness. Having a Sense of Urgency implies that you're completely present right now. All in all, you're aware of your present circumstance and are prepared to act expeditiously and conclusively. Despite the fact that not agonizing a lot over what may occur later on.

Having a need to keep moving will keep us from overthinking. All things considered, you center around the present, requiring each day in turn. A pioneer with a Sense of Urgency sees how quick moving the business world is. So the person endeavors to stay in front of every other person. To foster a desire to move quickly, you need a proactive methodology.

A proactive individual resembles a chess player. To win, you need to think a couple of strides ahead. The equivalent is valid in managing undertakings. To oversee time, you need to think ahead to perceive the main priority.

Control:

Direness begins in the psyche. Order requires enormous discretion. At the point when you are secured in your objectives, you will not get diverted.

Good faith and assurance:

Positive thinking gives certainty when circumstances become difficult, while assurance gives mental fortitude to continue to push ahead.

Conversation Time

The main piece of this preparation. Whoever's the big boss in the gathering should assign a facilitator, whose obligation is that every one of the inquiries you see on your screen is covered and that everybody, time allowing, can express their opinion.

Ensure all commitments are esteemed. All ideas considered, and all sentiments regarded.

Don't miss out!

Visit the website below and you can sign up to receive emails whenever B. Vincent publishes a new book. There's no charge and no obligation.

https://books2read.com/r/B-A-QWUO-FJGQB

BOOKS 2 READ

Connecting independent readers to independent writers.

Also by B. Vincent

Affiliate Marketing
Affiliate Marketing
Affiliate Marketing

Standalone
Affiliate Recruiting
Business Layoffs & Firings
Business and Entrepreneur Guide
Business Remote Workforce
Career Transition
Project Management
Precision Targeting
Professional Development
Strategic Planning
Content Marketing
Imminent List Building
Getting Past GateKeepers
Banner Ads
Bookkeeping

Bridge Pages
Business Acquisition
Business Bogging
Marketing Automation
Better Meetings
Conversion Optimization
Creative Solutions
Employee Recruitment
Startup Capital
Employee Mentoring
Servant Leadership

About the Publisher

Accepting manuscripts in the most categories. We love to help people get their words available to the world.

Revival Waves of Glory focus is to provide more options to be published. We do traditional paperbacks, hardcovers, audio books and ebooks all over the world. A traditional royalty-based publisher that offers self-publishing options, Revival Waves provides a very author friendly and transparent publishing process, with President Bill Vincent involved in the full process of your book. Send us your manuscript and we will contact you as soon as possible.

Contact: Bill Vincent at rwgpublishing@yahoo.com www.rwgpublishing.com